From Eleanor Harris
Xmas 1960

The Christmas Crib

1 *Stucco Crib Group by Francesco da Pietrasanta, in Santa Maria Maggiore.*

The Christmas Crib

BY

NESTA DE ROBECK

THE BRUCE PUBLISHING COMPANY
MILWAUKEE

NIHIL OBSTAT:

    JOANNES A. SCHULIEN, S.T.D.
    Censor librorum

IMPRIMATUR:

    ✠ ALBERTUS G. MEYER
    Archiepiscopus Milwauchiensis

    Die 9ᵃ Iulii, 1956

Rosary College Dewey Classification Number: 232.921

Library of Congress Catalog Card Number: 56-11151

Foreword

THE following pages are not a study of Crib art: they aim at making a little sightseeing journey to find out what Cribs have looked like in different countries and centuries.

This concerns all of us, for among what Mr. Henry Adams so happily calls our "two hundred and fifty million arithmetical ancestors" there surely must have been Crib enthusiasts in Italy, in Germany, in France, or England, or Spain. Some one of them may have helped to arrange a Presepio in Naples or have worked at Nativity altars in Germany or England, or acted in a Mystère in France. And why, please, should our ancestors be excluded from the company of those civilian pilgrims who must have been such an encumbrance to the Crusaders? I should like to think of one heaving up the heavy oak beams sent by Edward IV of England to re-roof the basilica of the Nativity in Bethlehem, or, best of all, let him have been among those privileged persons who listened open-mouthed to the story told by a Judean shepherd two thousand years ago.

Acknowledgments

I wish to acknowledge my indebtedness above all to Professore Rudolph Berliner's standard text book *Denkmaler der Krippenkunst* which contains pretty well all that is known about Christmas Cribs with most valuable illustrations; also to Signor Angelo Stefanucci, the foremost Italian Crib connoisseur and enthusiast, and founder of the Italian Crib Society who has most generously helped me with photographs; and not least to Messers Burns, Oates, Washbourne who have allowed me to make use of some of the material in my own book *The Christmas Crib* published by them and now out of print.

The Publisher also wishes to add his word of thanks to Rev. Aloysius S. Horn, Director of The American Christmas Crib Society, for his courtesy in supplying photographs of American cribs.

Contents

List of Illustrations

LIST OF ILLUSTRATIONS

The Christmas Crib

I

The Earliest Crib

EVER since the Incarnate Son of God was born in the cave
of Bethlehem Christians of each century and country have
wanted to represent the scene. We must, therefore, be prepared to find a great deal of variety in their representations.
A Crib may be very simple with all attention focussed on
the central figures; or it may be very elaborate, and that too
is justified because the whole world has to be gathered round
the manger.

Before deciding how to make our own Crib we want to
see what other people have done, and our first step is to turn
to Bethlehem where Crib history starts in that grotto and
manger which are spoken of in the Synoptic and Apocryphal
Gospels, by St. Justin Martyr, St. Epiphanius, and Origen
who says that he "saw the grotto and in it the manger where
Christ was swaddled." The Emperor Hadrian was so deter-
mined to smother the Christian tradition that he ordered a
wood to be planted and a sanctuary to Adonis to be built over
the place of the Nativity, and this profanation lasted until
A.D. 326 when the basilica of the Nativity was begun by St.
Helena and Constantine.

In his vivid letters St. Jerome describes Bethlehem and

2 *Grotto of the Nativity, Bethlehem. The Silver Star in the Pavement at the Left Marks the Place of Christ's Birth; the Altar at the Right, the Place of the Manger.*

3 *The "Salus Populi Romani," Picture in Santa Maria Maggiore, Said to Have Been Painted by St. Luke.*

4 *Reliquary of the Crib, in Santa Maria Maggiore.*

how he and his companions entered into the cave and adored "the place where the ox had known his Master and the ass the cradle of the Lord." However, he acknowledges one great disappointment: "if only I might have seen the Crib of clay in which the Saviour lay! Under pretext of honour we have substituted one of silver." Devotion has never been more cruelly misdirected! Perhaps some of the dust of the original manger mingled with the earth which was carried away by innumerable pilgrims who, according to St. Jerome and St. Augustine, journeyed to Bethlehem from every country.

Among these pilgrims Etheria, who was also an excellent sightseer, expatiates on the wonders of the churches of Golgotha and Bethlehem and on the services in which she took part. Other pilgrims, notably Anthony of Piacenza, Adamanno, Arculfo, and the Venerable Bede, speak of the Grotto as it was in the late seventh or early eighth century, its walls covered with marble and mosaic, and about this time the church was saved by a curious coincidence. During the Persian invasion the enemy noticed the Magi dressed in Phrygian cloaks and caps carved on the façade, and they took them for worshippers of Mithras bringing gifts to his altar. This mistake saved the church, but either the greed of the Persians or of warring Christian sects must have been at work for the silver Crib known to St. Jerome disappeared. But the grotto chapel of Bethlehem remains, one of the holiest places of our earth, with its silver star set in the pavement and the inscription: *"Hic de Maria Vergine Jesus Christus natus est."* — "Here Jesus Christ was born of the virgin Mary."

From Bethlehem we turn to Rome where the cult of the "Praesepe" began in the Basilica now known as Santa Maria

Maggiore, but whose original title was Sancta Maria ad Praesepe. Legend records that the site of the church was miraculously indicated on August 5, 352, when dwellers on the Esquiline were surprised to see part of the hill covered with snow. It was revealed to a Roman patrician and his wife that the Blessed Virgin desired a church to be built on this spot, and when it was discovered that Pope Liberius had had the same dream the church was immediately begun. Little trace, however, remains of the Liberian basilica; work on the present church was chiefly carried out under Pope Sixtus III in the middle of the fifth century. The church was dedicated to the Blessed Virgin in honour of the title "Mother of God" which had been decreed by the Council of Ephesus, and the great arch of the nave is decorated with scenes in mosaic referring directly to the maternity of our Lady. Only the Nativity is missing, an incomprehensible omission had there not existed a separate chapel commonly called the Domus Sanctae Dei Genetricis — the House of the Holy Mother of God. Tradition says that it was a crypt, probably built with stones from Bethlehem and copied from the original Grotto. Its chief treasure was a picture of our Lady and the holy Child, said to have been painted by the evangelist St. Luke. This wonder-working picture, which came to be known as the Salus Populi Romani, is the one crowned by Pope Pius XII in the Marian Year of 1954 and is still revered in Santa Maria Maggiore.

Gradually the "Domus" came to be known as the "Praesepe" (crib, manger), and similar chapels were erected in other churches; moreover, in the seventh century, the name "Praesepe" acquired new significance for it was then that the famous relics said to have been parts of the manger were transferred to Rome. It is impossible to be certain what the six small boards really were: we do know that St. Jerome and his friends in Bethlehem collected numerous relics, some of which passed to Constantinople and gradually found their way to the West. During the siege of Jerusalem Bethlehem was in great danger and St. Sophronius the Patriarch is thought to have sent the relics to Rome for safekeeping in the sanctuary of Sancta Maria ad Praesepe.

The first historical mention of the relics of the manger occurs in the eleventh century, but long before the Middle Ages the Praesepe chapel was being lavishly decorated with gold, silver, precious stones, and a wealth of costly ornaments. At Christmas the picture of our Lady was exposed upon the altar, and here the Pope celebrated the first Mass of the Nativity, the ceremonies continued throughout the night and the centre of the Roman Christmas was the Praesepe chapel. There is no doubt that the cult of the Crib took form first in Bethlehem, and then in Rome, and it has been said that there existed an ancient custom of placing figures in the manger. However that may be, it is evident from early Christian writings that the imagination of the faithful saw them there: let us try to recapture something of that imagination.

II

How the Story Was Told

FROM the earliest times Christians loved telling each other arresting tales about the Holy Family, and one cannot help wondering what was said by the great grandchildren of those who had actually heard the shepherds' story. Of countless legends some gradually solidified into the Apocryphal Gospels which St. Jerome denounced as the "deliramenta Apocriphorum," but what he condemned many of his followers enjoyed. They wanted to hear about the ass, and the ox bought by St. Joseph to sell in the fair, of the miraculous hay of the manger, of the cave filled with light at the entrance of our Lady, of the midwives being fetched by St. Joseph to testify to the Virgin Birth of Christ — a legend which naturally infuriated St. Jerome. They revelled in marvellous stories about the Magi and the adventures of the Holy Family during the Flight into Egypt regardless of whether they were fact or fiction, and these stories constantly reappear under different forms for a good fifteen hundred years.

The apocryphal legends have to be remembered, yet what tinsel they are, not only in comparison with the Gospels, but also with the writings of the Fathers and great Christian poets. St. Ephrem dwells on the mystical birth of Christ through the ages, the source of light and fruitfulness to all creation: he tells how first the shepherds come to worship Him who unites shepherds and sheep in one fold, of the field labourers adoring Him who has come to cultivate our fields, to fertilize our hearts and to take from them the seed of wheat for the eternal harvest, of the vintners worshipping the New Vine, the divine Vintner who will make all vines fruitful and all grapes sweet. The carpenters come to worship the foster Son of Joseph who has given man a new yoke; the newly married worship the Child of a Mother who is the Bride of the Holy Spirit, children come to welcome Him for their games who "hast brought the height of heaven down to the measure of Thy little ones." There follow the women and girls and this gathering of all people round the manger leads the way for what has become one of the chief characteristics of the Christmas Crib. St. Ephrem speaks of Christmas Day itself on an almost Franciscan note, the day which, like the Lord Himself, is the friend of young and old alike. Through all ages it returns each year, growing old with the old, renewed with the little child; each year it comes and passes, and comes again with unceasing joy. One of the loveliest passages is the invitation of the Eastern Christmas Office: "Come, o faithful, let us go and see where Christ is born, let us follow the star with the Magi, Kings of the East; a pastoral sounding of flutes is to give way to the songs of the angels, for what shall we offer Thee o Christ who for us hast appeared on earth as Man? Each of Thy creatures gives Thee thanks, the angels bring Thee a hymn; the sky a star; the Magi gifts; the Shepherds adoration; earth a grotto; the desert a manger; and we Thy Virgin Mother." The sanctity of the manger is beautifully sung by St. Ambrose, the manger out of which darkness was put to flight by new light: "O holy manger! Thy Crib eternal is sacred to all peoples for ever." In another hymn Prudentius exclaims, "Oh King of eternity how holy is the manger which serves as Thy cradle, venerated by all times and nations and even by dumb animals," and in a Eucharistic prayer St. John Chrysostom prays to Christ that "as Thou didst deign to lay Thyself down in the manger of a cave, so now deign to enter the manger of my sinful soul and defiled body."

We might quote many other similar passages from the great Greek and Latin writers in which the dramatic tendency is almost as marked as the lyrical. For those who could understand its full significance there was the sublime drama of the liturgy so rich in elaborate symbolism, while dialogues proved extremely useful for the expounding of the faith. A dialogue inevitably suggests dramatic action, and very early the Church had to face the question of how much or how little "action" could be permitted during the Christian services and especially during the homily. On this subject the Fathers were as divided as any later council on ecclesiastical discipline. With paganism still vigorous and the classical theatre an active, dangerous attraction, the Christian authorities wavered between sweeping condemnation and the desire to provide a counterinfluence and counterattraction. How insidious and powerful the influence of the theatre was we can gather from the repeated objections of the Church authorities to the popular songs, instruments, and dances which heretics tried to bring into Christian services. Some bishops were completely uncompromising, others slightly more tolerant. The Council of Laodicea decreed that only the clergy were to enter the pulpit and declaim and sing. Already the controversy over sacred drama had begun.

Happily the Church was able to fight the pagan theatre

not only with decrees but with the far stronger weapon of
the genius of her own writers, and in the great homily literature the Christian drama developed slowly but surely. The
lovely Canticle of St. Romanus of Emesa links together the
different episodes of the Nativity and it is impossible to read
it and not think of St. Bernard and Dante. It has a companion
in St. Romanus' beautiful Lament of our Lady beneath the
cross; if, as it has been suggested, these poems were generally
known and sung in Italy in the twelfth century, they may
even have been known to Jacopone da Todi, and may be
part of the background to his great Nativity and Passion
lauds. The sixth century homily included singing, recitation
by one or more persons, perhaps some action; the homilies
of such writers as Sts. Proclus, Basil, Efrem, or Gregory of
Nazianzus were to their time what the liturgical dramas,
mystery plays, and oratorios were to later centuries. They
appealed to the imagination and emotions quite as much
as to the intelligence of the audience which evidently was
in the habit of showing its feelings, else why was the deacon
told to call for order: "Silentium habete." No doubt necessary,
but an undemonstrative congregation would only have meant
an inattentive one.

It is uncertain how far the homilies were definitely "acted,"
but with them indisputably the liturgical drama was already
born. Gradually there developed a regular cycle of scenes
which became the stock-in-trade of every Nativity drama.
The scenes were roughly as follows: the Prophets, which
included passages from the Old Testament; a dialogue between God the Father and the Archangel Gabriel, in which
the latter is told not to alarm the Virgin; a soliloquy of
the Archangel before the house of Mary; the Annunciation
followed by a dialogue between Gabriel and Joseph after

5 *One of the Earliest Representations of the Magi (Third Century).
From the Catacomb of Domitilla.*

6 *The Magi From a Fourth-Century Sarcophagus.*

which the voice of God reassures St. Joseph. This part of the drama ends with a council of Devils. The second "act" opens with the journey of our Lady and St. Joseph to Beth-lehem, followed by the Nativity in the Grotto, the fetching of the midwives, the hymn of the angels, the adoration first of the shepherds, then of the Magi. It concludes with a scene representing the fury of the Devils. The final "act" has the Magi's visit to Herod, his consultation with his councillors, the massacre of the Innocents, the vision of St. Joseph and the Flight into Egypt, and the cycle is completed with the battle between Christ and the Devil with the final victory of our Redeemer. There is nothing immature in this ambitious spiritual drama which aimed at bringing home to literate and illiterate the facts of the Redemption.

We should like to know, of course, how these dramatic homilies were presented: St. John Chrysostom speaks of our Lady placing the Child in the manger and taking Him on to her knees; and St. Gregory Thaumaturgus finds the sight of the Crib the most eloquent comment on the Incarnation. "My eye," he says, "rests on the carpenter and cradle, on the young Child and His Mother. I see the Child lying in the manger while Mary the Virgin stands by serving with Joseph." These words were probably meant symbolically, and both in East and West, at least for a time, the altar was considered as the manger. But apart from the altar how was the scene represented; what did the audience actually see? Contemporary iconography helps us toward an answer.

III

The Crib of the Artists

IN SOME ways the Nativity was the easiest of Christian subjects, and the tendency of Graeco-Roman artists was to adapt to their Christian purpose what they saw around them. They generally show our Lady sitting under a shed, sometimes nursing her Son, or holding Him on her knees, but more often He lies in a basket-like manger between the ox and ass while the shepherds approach from one side and the Kings from the other.

With the waning of the Roman Empire iconography changed and the Byzantine tradition of the Grotto became paramount. Western eyes grew accustomed to seeing the Byzantine Nativity cycle presented in all the arts and it was pervaded by two currents of feeling, the transcendent and the human. Sometimes our Lady sits upright as though to show that the birth of Christ involved no human effort or suffering, or she may hold Him majestically on her knees as the Infant King: sometimes, especially in Carolingian art, the newborn Christ lies, not in a manger, but on the altar with the cross above Him or in His halo; or again He lies in a manger between the ox and ass while the Virgin reclines on a bed — an arrangement adopted to emphasize our Lord's

7 *An Early Medieval (Seventh Century) Ivory From Ravenna,*
Showing the Cycle of Nativity Scenes (Anderson).

humanity. Such variations were never simply the fancy of individual artists but were the expression of a definite theological point of view.

We find the recumbent Virgin already on the ivory throne in Ravenna, on the cross in the Sancta Sanctorum of St. John Lateran, or on the little phials of Monza. These latter are precious having been brought to Queen Theodolinda about A.D. 600, probably filled with earth from Bethlehem, water from the Jordan, or oil from some sanctuary lamp. They have Greek inscriptions and show the Nativity scene with the Magi wearing the famous Phrygian caps. Such phials and relics stimulated the fervour of those who could not travel; how eagerly they must have received the objects and listened to the tales of pilgrims more fortunate than themselves who could tell of the Christmas ceremonies in the Grotto of Bethlehem. Christians who could not reach Bethlehem in their Christmas services wanted to feel themselves there, and in some mosaics and paintings the figures are grouped in a Grotto obviously taken from descriptions of the cave of the Nativity.

It is certainly not to be wondered at that the human aspect of the Nativity should have asserted itself so forcibly. Tenderness is in each line of the Gospels and of the Fathers, and writers such as George of Nicomedia or Symeon Metaphrastes interpreted the gospel story in such a way as to foreshadow the Italian Trecento, while the Byzantine Baby can sometimes be seen hugging His Mother almost like a Della Robbia.

The age of the Baby is an interesting point: when He lies in the manger there is sometimes the suggestion of helpless infancy, but once on His Mother's knee He is often quite a large Child. Throughout the centuries few artists have

8 *A Monza Phial Showing the Annunciation to the Shepherds and the Magi (Seventh Century).*

9 *A Seventh-Century Gold-Glass.*

10 *Medieval German Nativity Scenes.*

faced the reality of the Creator of the universe as a newborn baby.

At first St. Joseph does not appear; when he does he is nearly always represented as an old man leaning on his stick; he is the Guardian.

Within a relatively short time the midwives become attendants who are seen giving the Child a bath, while the angels, besides filling the heavens with their praise, sometimes hold the star in place. There is also the very important scene of the annunciation to the shepherds, and in Byzantine art as also later, there is the clear individualization of the shepherds' response to the vision. The shepherds are shown as simple men in capes and hoods with their dogs, and one of them invariably plays a flute or a double pipe of reeds. This shepherd has come straight down from Arcadia; in classical art he was even crowned with flowers and the first earthly music to welcome the Christ Child was the "pastoral melody" of "shepherds skilled upon the tuneful pipes." The musician shepherd has always kept his place at the Crib, and does so still.

Until the thirteenth century the Magi were invariably Phrygians, who with cloaks blown out by the wind hurry forward holding their gifts, their pointed caps on their heads, and all more or less alike; in this, iconography took little heed of current legends.

No doubt it was the extraordinary richness of what we may roughly call Byzantine iconography of the Nativity which made its reign so long. In the finest work, as in rough provincial productions, the same scenes, the same gestures are repeated with choreographic order. When sufficient space was available the whole Nativity cycle was presented, otherwise the scenes were restricted to the Annunciation, the

Nativity, and Epiphany, and this cycle of scenes was made familiar in mosaic, in stone, in painting, gold, silver, ivory, and embroidery. A powerful spiritual impulse had produced a formula of vast range reaching from the homely to the heights of symbolical grandeur, a formula so highly charged with significance that it could lend distinction to even inferior compositions. The Christian impulse had infused new life into all the arts, uniting them in the service of that wonderful synthesis which is the liturgy.

The Nativity of Christ celebrated at the altar was represented on the walls, commented on in sermon and songs, and the dramatic representation of the Mystery became increasingly prominent in the Church services. Let us suppose ourselves back in some cathedral of Europe during the twelfth century: it is the Christmas season, and in the ceremonies of our Lord's birth we shall find the Christmas Crib.

IV

The Crib of the Liturgical Drama

THE Liturgical Drama of the West also developed from the homilies, but more immediately and obviously from the Tropes and Sequences in which Christian Latin poetry is so rich. This poetry went hand in hand with the wonderful flowering of Plain Song music: the Liturgical Drama was Music Drama, and to appreciate the full charm of the surviving texts one must hear them sung to their own lovely melodies.

The early Nativity Drama took place either before or after Matins or even formed an Introit to the Midnight Mass, and for it a veiled picture of our Lady and the Child was placed on the altar, or alternatively veiled figures, a light doing duty for the Star. The little scene was extremely simple, and it was acted by two groups of clerics representing the midwives and the shepherds. To the question: "Whom seek ye in the manger? shepherds say," the answer came: "We seek Christ our Lord, a Child wrapped in swaddling clothes according to the angel's word."

This basic dialogue was varied and enlarged according to local taste, and the culminating point was reached when the midwives pulled away the veil from the picture or figures

11 *The Nativity* (*Twelfth Century*) *at Chartres.*

12 *Pulpit Detail From Florence. The Lute Played by the Shepherd in the Foreground Is One of the Earliest Representations of That Instrument.*

announcing the birth of Christ to which the shepherds re-
plied with a threefold *Alleluia*.

Again the scenic arrangement is of special interest to us
in our search for the Crib, but it is not easy to be sure of
details. In later mediaeval times the altar did not always
represent the manger, which seems to have been a movable
object. In the vague stage directions it is generally mentioned
as something so well known as to need no description.
It seems reasonable to think that the Crib of the Dramas
resembled what we see in contemporary art: there does not
appear to have been any fixed rule either as regards the
construction or position of the Praesepe; probably it varied
according to the architecture of the Church. In Padua for
instance, it stood in the middle of the choir in front of the
altar; at Fleury near the door; in Rouen behind the altar of
the Cross. There was room for variety seeing that such dramas were acted from England to Sicily in every country
of Christendom.

Repeatedly we hear of an "imago" of our Lady and the
Holy Child being placed in the manger covered with a fair
linen cloth; sometimes figures were used, and marionettes
were already in vogue. There are suggestions, too, of human
actors; for instance Gerhard of Reichenberg speaks of a
"crying Child in the manger with His Mother."

At what date the ox and ass appeared as performers in
the dramas is uncertain, but they had always been present
in Nativity iconography and their presence was sanctified
by Isaias' prophecy — "The ox knoweth his owner, and the
ass his master's Crib" — and in the beautiful Christmas antiphon: "Oh great mystery and admirable sacrament that
God should lie in the manger between the animals." The
adoration of the Christ Child by all animals is a theme of

13 *Mosaic of the Nativity at Palermo. Note the Midwives in the Right Foreground Preparing to Bathe the Divine Child* (*see p. 32*) (*Anderson*).

the Apocryphal Gospels, and in parts of Spain the Midnight Mass was called the Mass of the Cock who, beating his wings cries, *"Christus natus est."* — "Christ is born." The ox, lowing, asks *"Ubi?"* — "Where?"; the goats and sheep bleat "Bethlehem" and the ass lifts up his voice with *"Eamus."* — "Let us go."

It was not long before the shepherds appeared in clothes suited to the part; they approached the Praesepe singing, *"Transeamus ad Bethlehem"* — "Let us go over to Bethlehem" guided by an angel, and after their dialogue with the mid-wives they remained in the choir during Mass in which they sang certain prayers and responses. At the end of the service the officiating priest turned to them with another question: "What have you seen, O shepherds, say; tell us what appeared to you on earth." To this they answered: "We saw God our Saviour born and round Him the choirs of angels. Alleluia." This dialogue was repeated during Lauds sometimes with additions and the shepherds reappear as guides of the Magi.

V

The Ordo Stellae in the Liturgical Dramas

WITH this Epiphany play the Nativity drama made a long stride forward in elaboration, but with the Praesepe as its centre. In the Middle Ages the numerous ancient legends had more or less crystallized, the number of the Magi was generally accepted as three and the twelfth century provided the familiar names of Melchior, Gaspar, and Balthasar. The fairly precise stage directions describe them: Melchior had to be old with a flowing beard and violet tunic and cloak; Gaspar, young and fair and beardless with a red cloak; Balthasar, dark of skin and hair in a red tunic, all the clothes to be of silk and cut on a Syrian pattern. The Magi must walk *"cum gravitate"* singing the antiphon *O quam dignis,* and before them must go a light representing the Star. Each of the Magi either bears his gift or has it carried by an attendant.

The different episodes were acted in different parts of the church, and the drama must have required considerable stage management. After the Magi's visit to Herod came the arrival in Bethlehem indicated by a light above the altar of the

39

14 *The Annunciation and Visitation From the Thirteenth-Century Psalter of St. Louis.*

15 *The Annunciation to the Shepherds (Twelfth Century), Paris.*

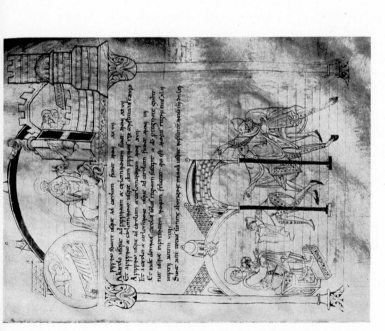

16 The Magi, St. Joseph's Dream, and the Flight Into Egypt, From an Eleventh-Century French Manuscript.

17 The Magi, From the Door of the Cathedral at Pisa.

Cross and when the Kings had found the Praesepe with the Mother and Child they prostrated themselves in adoration and offered their gifts singing the antiphon which told of gold for the divinity of Christ, incense for the true God, and myrrh for the suffering of His humanity. After this came the scene of their dream and departure.

The psychological clash between the Magi on one side and Herod and his councillors on the other brought a new note into the Drama, and before long Herod had become the regular stage villain, "furore accensus," according to one text, and the spectators were no doubt entertained to see him and his attendants untidily dressed and armed with wooden spears come bursting into the choir during Matins. Flinging his spear down Herod defiantly read one of the lessons while his attendants rushed about beating the clergy with inflated bladders.

Once popular comedy had entered the liturgical dramas it proved almost impossible to control. The original simple scenes were developed on more ambitious lines; other scenes were added, new characters appeared. In France especially it became the fashion to intersperse the Latin text with verses in the vernacular, and the Balaam incident in the scene of the Prophets developed into the riotous *Fête de l'Âne* — Feast of the Ass — just as the scene of the Holy Innocents led to the revels of the *Fête des Fous* — Feast of Fools — and the antics of the Boy Bishop. The elaborate stage of the Latin Liturgical Drama can best be studied in the Benediktbeurn text; with the various scenes it contains the original music, and probably lutes and pipes and the other instruments which appear in the sculptured Nativities were also used in the plays.

These were the dramas and this was the Praesepe known

42

18 *The Magi, Pistoia.*

19 *Adoration of the Magi. Mosaic in the Church of Santa Maria in Trastevere, Rome.*

to all the mediaeval saints and writers. Perhaps some of the clergy hoped that by allowing greater latitude to the plays these might provide a counterattraction to the Jongleurs' jovial performances in every fair, but the rowdiness of Herod, Balaam, and the Boy Bishop inevitably roused vehement opposition among stricter spirits. Protests were heard in many quarters: the wise abbess of Hohenburg wished to discriminate between ancient traditions "worthy of veneration," and unseemly "modern" innovations, and pointed out that everything depended on the spirit in which the play was performed. The old controversy between the Church and the theatre flared up again, and in 1207 Pope Innocent III in a letter to the archbishop of Gniesen denounced the dramas and condemned those who took part in them. A gloss added later in the century seems to indicate that the censure was not aimed at Nativity and Easter plays performed with reverence: still the Pope's Letter without the later gloss cannot have been without effect and it explains why St. Francis asked Innocent's permission to set up his Praesepe in Greccio for the Christmas of 1223.

VI

The Crib of Saint Francis

WITH St. Francis we come to a turning point in Crib history. Popular opinion is just as mistaken in thinking that he originated the custom of the Crib as it is in ascribing almost exclusively to him an attitude of tender compassion toward animals. Early Christian literature is full of tales illustrating the intimacy of saints and beasts; and in his youth Francis surely saw Nativity dramas and the then familiar iconography of the Nativity. His extraordinary originality lay in being able to transform and renew whatever he touched and to impress upon it forever the stamp of his unsullied genius and love.

Francis must often have prayed in the Praesepe chapels in Rome, and when he visited the Holy Places in 1220 something of himself will have remained there, but something of their spirit returned with him. For Francis Christmas had always been the "feast of feasts" bringing light and hope into a dark world, the day when "heaven and earth are made one" and "God condescended to be fed by human love." If Christmas fell on a Friday he swept aside fasting, wishing to see even "the walls rubbed with fat," every poor man entertained by the richer, and double rations given to every ani-

45

20 *St. Francis at the Crib, Greccio, 1223. Painting at Florence (Alinari).*

21 *The Franciscan Crib, Florence. These Two Paintings Are From the School of Giotto.*

mal, but especially to all oxen and asses. Could he but have
spoken to the Emperor the first favour he would have begged
would have been a decree ordering corn to be scattered on
the roads so that all birds, "but especially our sisters the
larks," should also feast.

The idea of celebrating the feast in a special way seems
to have occurred to him suddenly in the Advent of 1223.
He was in Rome and before leaving he asked the Pope's
permission to keep Christmas in his own way so as to realize
outwardly the poverty of Christ in the manger.

He sent for his friend Giovanni Vellita, a landowner of
Greccio where Francis had a favourite hermitage. "If now
it seems good to thee that we should celebrate this feast to-
gether, go before me to Greccio and prepare everything as
I tell thee. I desire to represent the birth of that Child in
Bethlehem in such a way that with our bodily eyes we may
see what He suffered for lack of the necessities of a newborn
Babe and how He lay in manger between the ox and ass."

Giovanni hastened to obey, and, says St. Bonaventure:
"Many brothers and good people came at Francis' bidding,
and during the night the weather also was beautiful. Many
lights were kindled, songs and hymns were sung with great
solemnity so that the whole wood echoed with the sound,
and the man of God stood by the manger, filled with the
utmost joy and shedding tears of devotion and compassion.
By his order the manger had been so arranged that Mass
was celebrated on it, and blessed Francis, the Levite of Christ,
sang the Gospel and preached to the people on the Nativity
of Christ our King, and whenever he pronounced His name
with infinite tenderness he called Him the "little Babe of
Bethlehem." St. Bonaventure, who certainly must have had
the account from an eyewitness, goes on to tell of the vision

of Giovanni who saw a Babe, seemingly lifeless in the manger until the Saint awoke Him out of sleep; and he comments: "nor was this vision untrue, for by the grace of God through His servant blessed Francis, Christ was awakened in many hearts where formerly He slept."

St. Francis' other biographer, Thomas of Celano, tells how "Greccio was transformed into a second Bethlehem, and that wonderful night seemed like fullest day to both man and beast for the joy they felt at the renewing of the mystery." He emphasizes the unusual consolation felt by the officiating priest, and the strong, sweet, clear voice of Francis as he read the Gospel and preached "saying all manner of tender things on the birth of the Poor King in Little Bethlehem. Repeatedly whenever he wished to name Jesus Christ, inflamed with immense love he called Him Babe of Bethlehem pronouncing the words almost like the bleating of a sheep, and his mouth seemed full, not only of his voice, but with emotion for when he named Jesus or Babe of Bethlehem, he licked his lips as though to taste the full sweetness of the words." Only an eyewitness could have given Thomas that detail.

This, then, was Francis' Nativity celebration; it had no connection with the Nativity Dramas in that he did not impersonate anyone, nor did the priest or brothers. There were neither the traditional figures nor dialogues, and there may or may not have been a figure in the manger. Nevertheless the Nativity of Our Lord was realized that night as fully as perhaps it ever can be. The love, the devotion, the concentration of each individual became one with that of Francis, and in Sabatier's words: "he was no longer in Greccio; his heart was in Bethlehem."

VII

The Influence of Saint Francis

ST. FRANCIS' Christmas at Greccio was not only an echo of Bethlehem or the expression of individual devotion evolved from older forms; in the fullest sense it was an augury of the future, and within a few years the Friars had carried it to every country of Europe.

St. Bonaventure says that Francis desired this particular celebration "to move the people to greater devotion," and moved they were to new enthusiasm and new joy. The Franciscan spirit gathered up all the old tendencies to stress the human and pathetic aspects of the gospel story and the least lettered could understand the Greccio Christmas Crib as well as any doctor of theology. It had an eloquence, a tenderness and single-minded simplicity of intention that the elaborate Nativity drama had lost. To those Umbrian peasants listening to Francis the Nativity of Christ must have been something as real as the birth of their own children: he gave into the arms of his followers that most precious of all babies, the Bambino Gesù.

From that moment the cult of the Christ Child is intensified: in the Franciscan world the Son of God becomes the loveliest of earth's children, the dear Little Lord Jesus who is everybody's Brother. We see Him throwing His arms round His Mother's neck while artists dwell caressingly on the perfect Baby's body that lies kicking in the straw or opening His eyes in delight at the sight of a bird held out by St. Joseph. The angels become lovely dimpled babies too, play-fellows who sing and play and offer Him fruit when they are not kneeling round the manger all "reverent, timid, and obedient." A new spring of poetic imagination had been released, and at its source stood Francis. On one point, how-ever, certainly the Italian painters and even the poets do not follow Francis who saw the newborn Christ in the reality of what that implies. We repeat: In art the age of the King of Heaven in Bethlehem is almost never that of a baby a few hours old.

The mark of Francis remained on every art; he who was one of the first of Italian poets writing in the vernacular was followed by any number of laud singers, and nativity lauds of Italy were first cousins to the carols of France and England, of Germany and Spain.

During the fourteenth century two other works appeared, both of major importance to Nativity poetry and iconography: *The Golden Legend* of James of Voragine, and the *Hundred Meditations* on the life of Christ probably by an Italian Franciscan. Of the two, *The Golden Legend* is on far the grander scale, and in the chapter on the Nativity the author repeats many of the older legends and also gives an account of the Sybil who had found her way into the Nativity Dramas together with the Prophets. It was she who, when the Em-peror was consulting her, showed him a golden circle round the sun in the midst of which was a beautiful Virgin holding a Child in her arms. And when the Emperor asked for an explanation of the vision he heard a voice saying: "This is

23 *The Nativity, by Fra Angelico, Florence. The Simple Tenderness of the Franciscan Spirit Is Evident in This Work* (Alinari).

the altar of heaven and this Child is greater than thou art, therefore we adore Him." This legend accounts for the foundation of the Ara Coeli church in Rome, and for the presence of a man and woman, the Emperor and the Sybil in many later Italian Cribs.

The Golden Legend also gives a vivid description of the Magi's journey which may well have served as the guiding text for a great Epiphany procession instituted by the Dominicans in Milan when different scenes were enacted at various points of the city. The Milanese could not forget that the relics of the Three Kings had been transferred from their church of Sant' Eustorgo to Cologne by the chancellor of Frederick Barbarossa.

The *Hundred Meditations* were even more popular than *The Golden Legend,* and though the book was intended only for the spiritual exercises of a Poor Clare nun it was read throughout Europe. It is full of tender human details, as for instance when it tells that the Little Lord Jesus was painfully circumcised which made Him and His Mother cry, but He gulped down His sobs because He could not bear to see her so sad. And the author admonishes the Poor Clare that she should emulate the adoration of the shepherds, "do thou likewise and ask His Mother that she may give Him to thee to hold and caress in thine arms, and look well on His face, and reverently kiss and be glad of Him. And this thou canst do in all confidence for He has come to dwell among sinners for their salvation." He also says that during the Christmas season not a day should pass in which Christians have not visited our Lady and her Son in the Crib while meditating on "their poverty and humility and great dignity."

To these we must add the Revelations of St. Bridget of Sweden who was also a follower of St. Francis, and who

24 The Shepherds, by Taddeo Gaddi. In the Church of
Santa Croce, Florence.

strikes the direct note of one who has seen and not only imagined a scene. She writes: "When I was present by the manger of the Lord in Bethlehem I beheld a Virgin of extreme beauty wrapped in a white mantle and a delicate tunic through which I perceived her virginal body. With her was an old man of great honesty and they had with them an ox and ass. These entered the cave and the man having tied them to the manger went out and brought in to the Virgin a lighted candle which having done he again went outside so as not to be present at the birth. Then the Virgin pulled off the shoes from her feet, drew off the white mantle that enveloped her, removed the veil from her head laying it beside her, thus remaining only in her tunic with her beautiful golden hair falling loosely over her shoulders. Then she produced two small linen cloths, and two woollen ones of exquisite purity and fineness which she had brought to wrap round the Child to be born, and two other small cloths to cover His head, and these too she put beside her. When all was thus prepared the Virgin knelt with great veneration in an attitude of prayer; her back was to the manger, her face uplifted to heaven and turned toward the East.

"Then, her hands extended and her eyes fixed on the sky she stood as in an ecstasy, lost in contemplation, in a rapture of divine sweetness. And while she stood thus in prayer I saw the Child in her womb move; suddenly in a moment she gave birth to her own Son from whom radiated such ineffable light and splendour that the sun was not comparable to it while the divine light totally annihilated the material light of St. Joseph's candle. So sudden and instantaneous was this birth that I could neither discover nor discern by what means it had occurred. All of a sudden I saw the glorious Infant lying on the ground naked and shining, His body pure from any soil or impurity. Then I heard the singing of the angels of miraculous sweetness and beauty. When the Virgin felt she had borne her Child immediately she worshipped Him, her hands clasped in honour and reverence saying: 'Be welcome my God, my Lord, my Son.'

"Then, as the Child was whining and trembling from the cold and hardness of the floor where He was lying, He stretched out His arms imploring her to raise Him to the warmth of her maternal love. So His Mother took Him in her arms, pressed Him to her breast and cheek, and warmed Him with great joy and tender compassion. She then sat down on the ground laying the Child on her lap and at once began to bestow on Him much care tying up His small body, His legs and arms in long cloths, and enveloped His head in the linen garments, and when this was done the old man entered, and prostrating himself on the floor he wept for joy. And in no way was the Virgin changed by giving birth, the color of her face remained the same nor did her strength decline. She and Joseph put the Child in the manger, and worshipped Him on their knees with immense joy until the arrival of the Kings who recognized the Son from the likeness to His Mother."

We cannot leave "Bride's Book" without remembering its English reader, Margery Kempe, that enthusiastic pilgrim who was in the Holy Land early in the fifteenth century and recorded her sensations at length. Her keen imagination was perhaps an exception to the general rule; nevertheless carols, lauds, plays, pictures, and sculptures prove how many people were sufficiently like her to account for some of the most attractive passages and details of contemporary art and literature. They all contributed to the Christmas Crib.

VIII

The Crib in Renaissance Art

TOWARD the end of the thirteenth century Arnolfo di Cambio was entrusted with the restoration of the Praesepe chapel in Santa Maria Maggiore, and at that time the body of St. Jerome was translated from Bethlehem to the celebrated chapel in Rome. Little now remains of Arnolfo's design except the figures of the Kings for a Nativity group, some of the very earliest of their kind. These prove to us that the Crib was beginning to assert itself as an independent entity, although the chief development still lay with sculpture, painting, and the ubiquitous plays.

Nothing in Nativity iconography is more striking than the difference in the bas-reliefs of Nicola and Giovanni Pisano, working in Pisa also in the later thirteenth century, close to each other in date, far apart in spirit. Nicola's Nativity is classical, his figures full of a pagan pride and self-reliance that would certainly never have sought a King in the "rich poverty of the manger." Giovanni was influenced by French iconography: the Christ Child lies in the manger between the ox and ass, while His Mother leans forward and tenderly uncovers His face for it is she who shows Him to the world. We notice, too, a midwife dipping her finger into

25 *Figures of the Magi, Among the Earliest of Their Kind. Made for
a Crib Group by Arnolfo di Cambio, Santa Maria Maggiore.*

26 *Bas-Relief by Giovanni Pisano.*

the bath to feel the temperature of the water. Orcagna presented the new gestures with even greater beauty and we find ourselves before another interpretation of the Nativity scene. The Byzantine Grotto gradually disappears, the humanity of our Lord has become so explicit that there is no need for the recumbent position of the Virgin. Once the match had been set to this train of imagination it spread like wildfire as we see in the various Books of Hours, in the *Bible des Pauvres* and the *Speculum Humanae Salvationis*. Here no detail is too human or too small and we revel in them together with the artists. The scene of the annunciation to the shepherds comes to the fore, rich in possibilities, the landscape gains in importance and the Saviour is surrounded with the sun shining on fields and water, luminous mountains fading into the distance, while trees in leaf rustle in the breeze, rabbits skip in the grass, and all creation smiles in the light of the Redemption.

If the northern artists revelled especially in the Nativity and Holy Infancy, the southerners revelled even more luxuriantly in the Epiphany. Painters who had probably tried their hands successfully as stage managers saw the procession of the kings as a gorgeous theatrical "trionfo." Charmed as they were by the increasing pageantry of Renaissance life they set the Epiphany in the sumptuous world of courts with everyone dressed in marvellous and most expensive clothes. It was the feast of all that was most elegant when kings of France got themselves painted as the Magi in whose honour Jean le Bon instituted an order of chivalry.

Throughout the Renaissance imposing dramatic processions were the fashion: by the end of the fourteenth century the papal censure had been forgotten and Mystères in France, Mystery Plays in England, Sacre Rappresentazioni in Italy,

27 *The Nativity, and the Adoration of the Magi,*
by Orcagna, Florence.

28 *The Nativity, by Andrea della Robbia, Siena. This Work Shows Strong Franciscan Influence.*

29 *A Fifteenth-Century Flemish Crib.*

30 *Begarelli's Crib (Sixteenth Century) at Modena.*

31 *The Visit of the Magi. Bas-Relief at Verona. This Is Companion Panel to the one Shown at the Bottom of Page 68.*

Misterios in Spain, Geistliche Schauspiele in Germany were flourishing with renewed vigour. The reciprocal influence of the plays and the plastic arts is everywhere apparent. Just as the Middle Ages had carved the scenes of its dramas on the façades and doors and pulpits of its cathedrals, so the Renaissance took its version of the same scenes and set them on screens and in the reredos to its altars.

We have only to think of the great screens in France where in the cathedral of Chartres, for instance, the life of Christ was illustrated with more than two hundred figures, or the beautiful alabasters of England, or the great carved and painted altars of Germany. The German Nativity altar with the Crib as its centre was often simply called "Bethlehem." The retablos of Spain went still further in grandeur and elaboration, and Italy had Nativity altars, generally of more modest proportions.

The Della Robbia family made a number of these altars, and Andrea especially is a poet of the Nativity in the pure Franciscan tradition. The Della Robbia Nativity is nearly always restricted to the manger with the adoration of the Shepherds, the apparition of the angels being placed in the background. It is almost a protest against the elaboration of other works. The Visitation figures at Pistoia give us a pang of regret for what a full Nativity group might have been.

Nativity altars in majolica became popular, no doubt partly owing to their relative cheapness, and sometimes stucco figures stand out against a painted background as in Volterra. Pietro da Pietrasanta made a lovely group of stucco figures for Santa Maggiore in Rome, Guido Mazzoni one for Modena cathedral, rather later Begarelli who was also a successful stage manager, made another for Modena, and Brandani one for an oratory in Urbino.

32 *Nativity Altar by Hans Degler, Augsburg.*

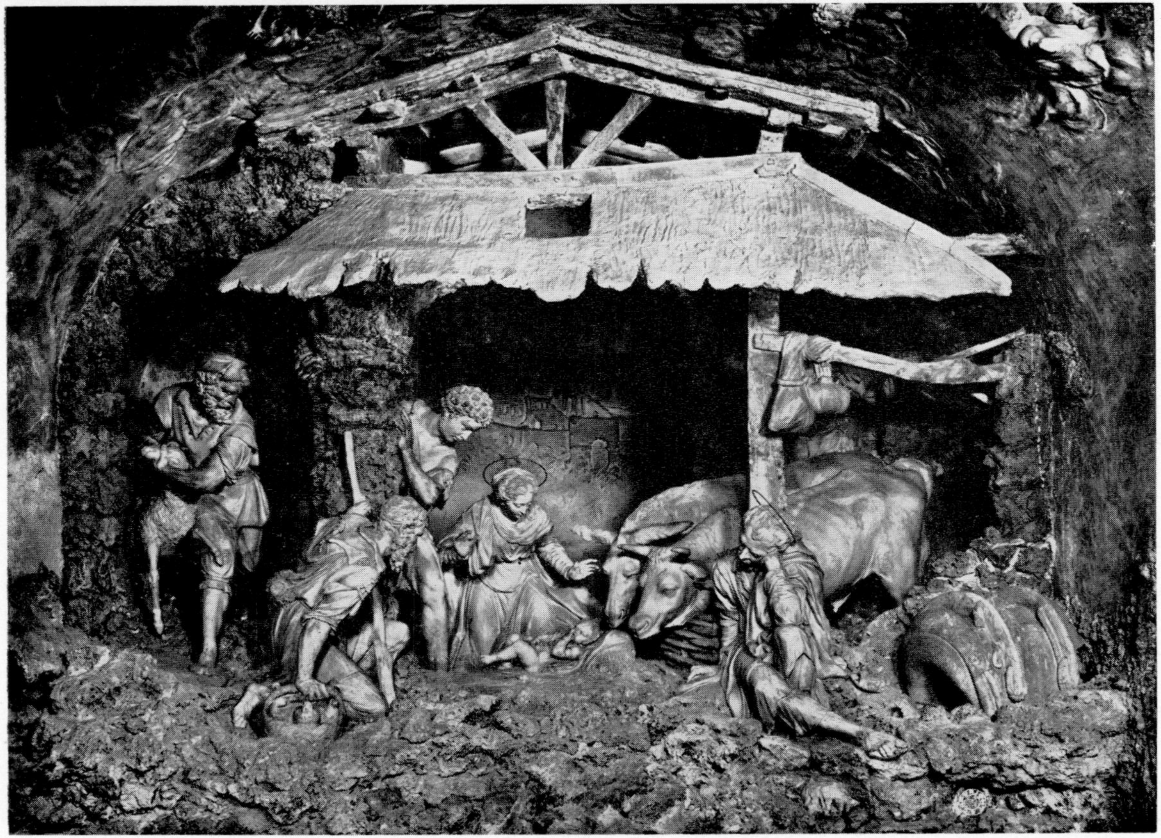

33 *The Brandani Crib, at Urbino.*

Another custom was that of placing groups of figures in shrines or chapels, often near a Franciscan convent, scattered about a wooded hill which became a Sacro Monte where pilgrims could follow the life of our Lord or some saint in the groups of life-size figures each representing a particular scene. It was a still life and devotional mystery play. The earliest Sacro Monte was that of San Vivaldo in Tuscany where the Nativity and some other groups were by the Della Robbias, but by far the most ambitious was the rather later Sacro Monte of Varallo where our Lord's life was presented in fifty chapels, eleven of them dealing with the Nativity cycle, the work of Gaudenzio Ferrari and other artists.

Throughout this time the idea of the Crib as something independent was asserting itself in every country, and the medieval name "Praesepe" became *Crib* in England, *Crèche* in France, *Krippe* in Germany, *Presepio* in Italy, *Belem* in Portugal, *Nacimento* in Spain. Carden on the Moselle has a remarkable group of figures of the Magi belonging to the mid-fifteenth century: there are wooden figures of our Lady seated on the ass with the Christ Child in the Emmerich Museum, obviously the Flight into Egypt, while dusty old prayer books contain hymns and devotions "to be sung in front of the Crib."

A remarkable group of figures at Chaource gives an idea of a French crèche; another is at Sainte Marie d'Oleron in the Pyrenees, yet another at Nogent-le-Rotrou, and at Aube-voye in the Eure the Cardinal de Bourbon, uncle of Henri IV, built a chapel whose crypt was copied from the Grotto at Bethlehem. In France as elsewhere the earlier figures were either of carved and painted wood, or sometimes gilt as at Saint Maximin du Var, or they were of modelled and painted clay; china was used later while the Orleans museum has a

34 The Nativity (Fifteenth Century) in Volterra. The Figures Are by Rosellino; the Background by Benozzo Gozzoli.

35 The Magi, Volterra.

36 Remaining Figures From the Crib by Alemanno. Made for
San Giovanni dei Carbonari, Naples, in 1478.

37 Nativity Altar, Verona.

38 Barocci's Nativity (Sixteenth Century), Madrid.

collection of glass, wax, and wrought iron cribs.

It is, however, to Italy that we must turn for more numerous early Cribs, and tradition says that the custom has always existed in the Basilica of St. Francis in Assisi. There are signs of it in many places of Umbria, Tuscany, and the Marches, and especially in Naples when we first hear of a Crib given to the church of Santa Chiara by Sancia, wife of Robert of Anjou. Then in 1438 eleven figures were carved by Martino de Jadena for the church of Sant' Agostino Maggiore and a little later Giovanni Alemanno was commissioned for a Presepio of forty-eight figures for San Giovanni dei Carbonari and a few have survived as has the Presepio made by Giovanni da Nola for San Giuseppe dei Falegnami. Another was made for Montoro, the nuns of the Sapienza asked Annibale Caccavello for fourteen figures, while Pietro di Bergamo was commissioned for twenty-eight figures for the church of San Domenico Maggiore and they were set in a grotto hollowed from stones said to have been brought from Bethlehem.

The fourteenth and fifteenth centuries were feeling their way toward the Crib as we know it; but still where it was always to be found was in the Mystery Plays of England, the Mystères of France, the Sacre Rappresentazioni of Italy, the Misterios of Spain, the Geistliche Schauspiele of Germany.

IX

The Nativity
Plays of the Renaissance

WHEN the religious plays returned from their temporary exile they were no longer the Latin Liturgical Dramas, but plays in the vernacular, rich in local customs. In Italy, for instance, they emerged among the Laud singers of Umbria, Tuscany, and the Abbruzzi in the form of a dramatic "Devotion." Sometimes there was more sermon and less action, sometimes the reverse. A platform near the pulpit served as a stage. Nazareth, Jerusalem, Bethlehem were indicated by a signboard, while journeys had to be imagined until the plays became more ambitious and demanded the whole church.

Before long the preaching was set aside and the more popular elements of the Liturgical Drama were revived and continued. Some plays were directly influenced by the *Hundred Meditations*: everyone, no matter how poor had acquired the right to look into the divine nursery of Bethlehem to help in holding the Baby, in bathing and dressing Him, and St. Joseph is made busy in many domestic chores.

Especially in the north the Crib took the form of a regular

39 Mechanical Crib (Sixteenth Century) Made by Hans Schlottheim for the Court of Saxony. Now in Dresden (Description, p. 81).

40 Seventeenth-Century Crib, by Stammel.

41 *Angel From the Eighteenth-Century Crib of the Ursulines at Bozen.*

42 *English Alabaster Nativity.*

43 *Eighteenth-Century German Crib. Now in the National Museum, Munich.*

cradle, the best that money could buy since it was to serve for a King. Some stood on rockers, some were suspended to side posts like that known as the cradle of Charles V in Brussels, and if possible it contained a relic of Bethlehem. In the Beguinages of Flanders, in convents and pious families such cradles were habitual, the little King's sheets were marvels of needlework, and fringes of silver bells tinkled for His delight. If the cradle stood in a church, the rocking of it became part of a service performed by the clergy and congregation singing appropriate lullabies.

Noels and carols sang of scenes from the apocryphal Gospels, and these were repeated with ever increasing elaboration in the plays. The Office de l'Ane (Drama of the Ass) was expanded into the streets as well as churches while each year the scene of the inn became more rowdy, to contrast with the arrival of one poor family for whom none had room.

The shepherds appeared bringing gifts from their own provinces, cloth from Flanders, grapes from Burgundy, truffles from Perigord, while the bitter hardships of an Appennine winter echo in the Abbruzzi play when the shepherds offer the Madonna their own cloaks, apologizing if they smell of goats, and turn to the audience with the words: "Think how the Blessed Virgin had not so much as a sack or cloth to protect her, nor fire to warm the icy air, and that the Lord of the world had neither mattress nor cushion on which to lie, nor garment in which He might be wrapped."

In Tuscany the shepherds and their dogs have names, and they bring wood and cheeses and chestnuts, while Randello, who is the musician, plays the bagpipes and offers a flute or pipe to the Bambino. On their way to the manger the shepherds sometimes meet the Devil who tries to turn them aside, and when they arrive St. Joseph greets them, the benevolent father of the family. There is no reference to the theme of his doubts of the Blessed Virgin which evidently offended Italian taste but can be met in English Mystery plays of the same period. When the shepherds leave the manger they often meet the Kings and the midwives with their children and an animated street scene follows further enlivened by a crowd of beggars who are given the characteristically Franciscan name of the "Little Poor of the Lord."

In every country the stage manager of the plays was a great personage; he was responsible for training the actors, often men and boys belonging to a Confraternity, and his reputation depended on the novelty and excitement he was able to produce, if not in the plot, at least in its presentation. The more ambitious plays had heaven and hell on higher and lower levels from the platform where the action was performed, and the more revolving lights and flowers there were in heaven, and the more vivid the Devil belching smoke and swallowing sinners into immense jaws, the better the public was pleased. Fifteenth-century Parisians were delighted with "un enfer noir et puant" — "a hell black and stinking."

Many great Renaissance artists were quite ready to design Court pageants and "triumphs," allegorical intermezzi and mystery plays, and Brunelleschi is credited with having adapted the "mandorla" to scenic purposes. It was an oval framework adorned with lights and flowers and was convenient for letting down actors and lifting them up and thus varying entrances and exits. A picture by Carpaccio shows a church prepared for a Sacra Rappresentazione which might also be combined with a procession in which case it was enacted practically all over the city. In Florence Feo Belcari and Lorenzo il Magnifico wrote plays which the Medici

44 *The Magi, by Bartolo di Fredi, Siena. The Pageantry Inspired
by the Renaissance Nativity Plays Is Evident Here.*

children helped to act, and particular occasions were marked by especially gorgeous plays. Macchiavelli describes one Epiphany drama which gave work to everyone for six months, adding what was perhaps true that Lorenzo encouraged such shows to keep people's minds off politics. It is well known that Benozzo Gozzoli's frescoes in the Riccardi chapel show the chief personages who gathered in Florence for the Council of 1439: a further point of interest is that the magnificent clothes worn by these grand people correspond pretty closely to those used by a guild of Laud Singers, to which Giuliano dei Medici belonged. The play was held in the church and cloister of San Marco and was subsidized by the authorities.

Mantua, too, staged a splendid Sacra Rappresentazione with so many lights that Isabella d'Este recorded her alarm, and what the Gonzagas did in Mantua, the Estes did in Ferrara, the Montefeltros in Urbino, and the Visconti in Milan none of whom were going to be outdone by Florence. In Modena another most elaborate Nativity drama was staged by Begarelli.

In Naples, too, the plays had an immense vogue from puppet shows at street corners to dramas such as that of Aversa which took a week to perform and covered the whole life of our Lord. In these dramas devotional feeling was inextricably mixed with local customs and superstitions; no one was to be excluded from Bethlehem, not even the gypsy who had come to tell the Bambino's fortune and give Him a pot of honey. The Neapolitan plays were entitled the "Monarca dei Matti" (Monarch of Fools) and the "Vescovello" (Boy Bishop) and some scenes so closely resembled the Fête des Fous as to suggest that during the Angevin rule the French plays had become familiar to the Neapolitans.

Spain, too, was greatly given to Nativity plays by such

authors as Gil Vicente, Inigo de Mendoza, and Lope de Vega: nearly always the Spanish Nativity was graver than the French or Italian, but there as everywhere protests were again being heard, and again opinion was divided. Sant' Antonino the archbishop of Florence forbade his clergy to take any part in the buffooneries of the mystery stage, and demanded that if there were to be dramas in the churches they must be devotional: St. Charles Borromeo the archbishop of Milan went further, and as to Savonarola he denounced all plays in terms that would have done credit to Tertullian. The tide was flowing in favour of the strict, and the Council of Trent put an end to the plays in churches, but not before a number of serious fires had occurred. The churches indeed, were no longer adapted to the type of performance the Mystery Plays had become, and gradually everywhere they were transferred to cloisters, squares, or other buildings. Thus the plays disappeared from the churches, but they left there the central point of interest and their very raison d'être, the Christmas Crib.

X

The Later Crib

HAD we been in Rome for the Christmas of 1517 we might
have been present at the Mass of St. Gaetano of Thiene in
the Presepio chapel of Santa Maria Maggiore when he saw
in the manger a living Child Who was put into his arms by
the Madonna, while in a vision he followed all the scenes
of the Infancy. After this St. Gaetano never failed to set up
a Crib, using it as his pulpit and often inviting shepherds
to come with their bagpipes. St. Charles Borromeo and St.
Philip Neri both loved and venerated the Presepio chapel
where St. Ignatius said his first Mass; and as to Pope Sixtus
V he could not rest until he had had it completely restored.
The century which sanctioned the demolition of the old St.
Peters had no qualms about radical changes to the Presepio
chapel of Santa Maria Maggiore, and very little of the original was left.

The very serious devotion of the Counter Reformation
brought deep understanding to the Nativity; the elaborate
clothes and processions disappeared, the manger is that of
any stable, and the only light streams from the newborn
Child and shines first of all on His Mother Who adores
Him lying in the manger or on the edge of her cloak. Devo-

45 *Crib Originally in the Ursuline Church at Bozen.*
Now in the National Museum, Munich.

46 *An Eighteenth-Century South German Crib,*
National Museum, Munich.

tion to our Lady rose in fervour with every attack on her unique position.

All this contributed to the popularity of the Christmas Crib and the demand for Cribs came both from churches and from private families. Even in the fifteenth century the Visconti of Milan had one, and a century later Buontalenti in Florence arranged a Presepio for his pupil Francesco, the son of Cosimo de' Medici, first Grand Duke of Tuscany. In this the heavens opened, angels flew about and came down to earth and the figures "walked toward the holy Manger assuming attitudes which seemed entirely natural." It is unkind of fate to lose Buontalenti's mechanical Crib which may have been inspired by the Three Kings on the clock tower of Venice.

At Munster Hans Brabender made a still grander clock-work Crib where the Magi bowed to the Christ Child while the clock played a hymn. But the most ingenious mechanical Crib was perhaps that now in the Dresden museum which was made about 1589 by Hans Schlottheim of Augsburg as a present to the Elector Christian I from his wife Sophia. The lower part has a clock and silver gilt plaques showing scenes from Bible history, from designs of the medallist Stephanus Delaune: the scenes are divided by statuettes of the Apostles and two other figures of a Roman soldier and a weeping woman recall the Massacre of the Innocents. The second tier is roofed like a house, and above again on four brackets is a sphere with embossed and engraved signs of the Zodiac and the northern constellations. When the clock was wound the globe opened showing God the Father surrounded by angels, while part of the wall on the second tier slid back and the manger appeared: the Angels then descended from heaven; to a well-known carol tune, St. Joseph rocked the

47 *Another South German Crib of the Eighteenth Century,
National Museum, Munich.*

cradle, the ox and ass rose from their knees, while the shepherds and kings passed before the manger. Surely the children of the Saxon court were only allowed to enjoy such a plaything on Sundays!

Other German-speaking royal children were also enjoying Cribs, and a Bavarian princess Maria married in Graz wrote to her brother in Munich in 1577 asking for a painted and carved ox and ass; then she thanks him for eight angels, and yet again for four shepherds, three Kings, a servant, St. Joseph, and "old Simeon." This good lady had fifteen children and says "little Anna means to complain that she cannot keep the ox and ass for her very own" so her mother suggests that an extra pair should be sent: "if you really want to give them to her, let them be large and very strong for they will have to stand a lot of hard wear." She specifies that the figures are to have stuff clothes: "I don't care much for figures carved and painted, and they are horribly expensive and I am horribly poor." She repeats the injunction two years later when she orders our Lord, our Lady, the twelve Apostles, adding that the figures must be jointed, and able to stand, sit, and kneel "which should be quite easy if they are properly made with wire." Another order for trumpeters was sent four years later. One of the children for whom this Crib was made was afterward Kaiser Ferdinand I, a champion of the Counter Reformation. Another brother who was studying for the priesthood in Ingolstadt sent his brothers and sisters a new Crib with a special carpenter from Munich to set it up. Other records show Crib entries: clothes for different figures are ordered, the wages paid to sewing maids, carvers, and painters, and from the fifteenth century onward the Crib had been welcomed into homes of all kinds. The mystery of Christmas must have been emphasized for German children

48 *Section of Crib by Moser (Nineteenth Century). The Artist's Emphasis on Architecture Can Be Noted (p. 109), National Museum, Munich.*

49 *Crib by Mayr, Showing the Influence of Nineteenth-Century German Romanticism.*

by the habit of making Nativity altars to shut like cupboards, then with the opening of the doors the Crib was made visible. Crib making has always appealed to the German genius for toys, and also to that deep sentiment only to be described as the "Weihnachtsstimmung," and in both Catholic and Protestant Germany the "Krippen haüslein" has always stood beneath the Christmas tree, completed by the singing of that loveliest of all carols the *Heilige Nacht*.

In the seventeenth century no one understood the value of the Crib better than the Jesuits, and wherever they went in Germany their churches inevitably had Cribs which were sometimes extended into including the whole Christian Year rather like a miniature Sacro Monte. Naturally each convent had its Crib which, unluckily, were nearly all dispersed during the dissolution of the religious orders. One, formerly belonging to the Servite nuns near Innsbruck, is now in the Munich Museum; it is the typical grand German rococo Crib with many scenes and wonderful trappings round its exquisite dolls.

Many German churches possess detailed accounts of their Cribs, generally of the seventeenth and eighteenth centuries, and everywhere Crib making was a lucrative occupation to a number of people; in the Bavarian and Austrian Alps whole families specialized in the carving of large Crib figures just as much as for tiny Cribs to travel with their owner. They still continue today.

The Crib artists of Germany were extremely numerous: in the sixteenth century Hans Krauth and Theodor Goth were well-known potters. Then Munich asserted itself as a centre of Crib art and there are admirable figures by Niklas, Knoller, Boos, an animal specialist, by Gunther, a famous Baroque artist renowned for his angels, by Schuster and

Nissl, Schwanthaler and Kieninger and Giener, all of them artists of marked individuality. With the advent of the dressed doll, miniature painters such as Hans Kager and Hans Schor were called in for the delicate work on faces and hands: it was Absam who introduced the landscape of Palestine as his Crib background and in him and Mayr the Crib of German romanticism found its chief exponents.

Each part of Germany produced elaborate baroque and rococo Cribs, but alongside of these, as in no other country, there were Cribs of genuine folk art with their traditional dress, customs, and material. And longer than anywhere else the Christmas marionette show, the *Krippenspiel,* drew crowds in the fairs, especially in Austria, unaware no doubt that they were witnessing the last echo and survival of the Mystery Plays.

Germany is a fascinating country for the Crib lover, but we must turn back to the South.

XI

The Later Crib in the South

Italy

WITH the dawn of the seventeenth century the making of Presepi had become a recognized trade in Naples, and the artists and craftsmen engaged in it were commonly known as "Figurari." They too were numerous and among the first group the most famous were Vaccaro, Falcone, and Somma: crib figures, generically known as "pastori" were becoming a little world to themselves. The earliest Neapolitan cribs had all been fixed groups of statues; but a new technique was introduced when Vaccaro made a set of figures for Santa Maria in Portici which were dressed in stuff clothes.

From that moment the Figurari tended to discard the solid figure in favour of the puppet with a body of rags wound on wire, and feet, hands, and head exquisitely modelled, then baked, coated with size, and painted. The finish of every tiny detail was accentuated when the Figurari became employed in the china factory of Capo di Monte which had been transferred at one time to Spain but was brought back to Naples. Some of the Figurari were invited to work in Spain taking with them Italian models, bringing

50 *Neapolitan Crib of the Eighteenth Century.*
Now in Museum of Cluny, Paris.

back Spanish ones. When a Neapolitan King married a Saxon princess there came in designs from the Meissen factory, and again other Figurari found work in Germany.

The advent of the puppet started a whole series of new trades, chief among them the dolls' dressmaker, and as in Germany the modelled and painted figure and the dressed puppet existed side by side. In the eighteenth century Naples is reputed to have had four hundred Presepi in its churches, and many private houses also had their "Bethlehem" on which the owners spent large sums, encouraged to do so by a famous Dominican preacher, Padre Rocco, who made the Presepio his special theme. He was a father to all the outcast and poorest of Naples: when the police did not dare to light the streets for fear of the Lazzaroni, Padre Rocco appealed to his friends on the ground that it was a public disgrace to leave the Madonna in her shrine alone in the dark. The streets were lighted. Padre Rocco found time to rush from house to house spurring on laggards and among his enthusiastic followers were the Kings Carlo III and Ferdinando IV. The King superintended his own Presepio and the whole court was kept busy: each detail for the puppets, each tiny ribbon or flower or buckle was carefully planned, and some of the stuffs were especially woven as when one of the Magi wore a mantle which was an exact reproduction of that worn by Carlo III as Grand Master of the Order of San Gennaro.

Very quickly the Presepio became a genre picture of Neapolitan life; often it was as theatrical as any Mystery Play, presented by artists fully equipped in the elaborate stagecraft of the time, accustomed to design and arrange the magnificent secular and religious Triumphs which were then so popular. Often they represented the complete Nativity cycle of scenes, but above all the episodes of the shep-

51 *The Neapolitan Inn (Eighteenth Century), Agresti Collection, Naples.*

herds, the Magi, and the Inn. While the shepherd puppets were being put in place, real shepherds from the mountains of the Lazio and Abbruzzi could be seen in the streets of Naples throughout the Christmas Novena, and three times every day with flute and bagpipes they went the round of all the shrines of our Lady to serenade her and "console her for all she suffered on the road to Bethlehem."

The scene of the inn gave the Figurari a chance they certainly made the most of; there could be seen every variety of maccaroni and fish, sausages and wines from Ischia or Capri, while a countryman unloads a cart of vict- uals, a salesman displays his goods, beggars hold out a hand, minstrels play the guitar or hurdy-gurdy, and the guests eat and drink and gamble. It is an "Allegro con brio" from a Neapolitan opera and is continued in the procession of the Kings decked out like princes from the Arabian Nights, laden with jewelled gifts, accompanied by slaves, camels, elephants, monkeys, horses, birds, and dogs, and this colorful cavalcade was completed by another of beautiful eastern princesses known as Georgine. The great ladies and gentle- men of Naples were to be found in the Crib alongside every kind of person from every province, cityfolk and coun- tryfolk, all dressed in the right clothes, and in a setting which included every conceivable object known to daily life, each and all represented in perfect miniature models. No wonder that the Presepio gave work to such a host of people, of all the professions and arts.

Many of the private Presepi took up a number of rooms in a house. In that of the lawyer Signor Rafaello Sorvello the crowd was so great that guards had to keep order. Signor Terres in his showed the most topical and latest scenes, that of Don Sdanghi was the work of a lifetime and he would

52 The Inn of Another Neapolitan Crib, Catelli Collection, Naples.

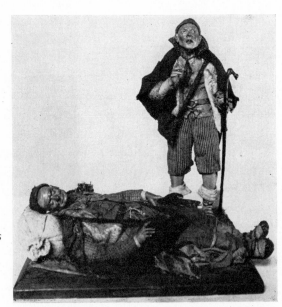

53 Two of Sammartino's
Shepherds, Giusto
Collection, Naples.

54 An Eighteenth-Century Neapolitan Crib, on Which Several Artists Collaborated.

not sell it even to the King. It is now in Munich.

At first sight the Presepio of Naples may appear a magnificent toy, but to see it only in this light is to miss the point. It is missionary in spirit and intention, and also in presentation. The Christmas Crib can be that of Bethlehem, but it can also represent the extension of the Incarnation in the whole world among men of all lands and avocations. Throughout the centuries we have seen how many people who could not travel wanted to feel themselves present in Bethlehem, at any rate in their Crib: the Neapolitan Figurari to a hitherto undreamed of degree brought Bethlehem to Naples, or took the whole of Naples to Bethlehem. This was certainly due to Padre Rocco.

It was friendship with this Dominican which first brought the court painter Celebrano to making puppets. His figures give very much the impression of having been taken from life: there is a certain type of bald shepherd, or of rugged face which is unmistakably his, as well as elegant courtiers. His friend Gori liked the comfortable, well-fed steward with a stout pleasant wife and another favourite artist, Mosca, in his spare time from being a clerk in the Ministry of War made excellent studies of countryfolk as well as models of Neapolitan farms and other buildings. With Mosca there worked Tozzi, a painter in the Capo di Monte Factory and a specialist in hands, no matter whether molded by ease, work, or suffering; hands as individual as the temperaments of their owners.

The animals of the Presepio also had their specialist Gori, who besides portraying his patrons would also model some favourite horse or dog, then there were Vassallo, and Saverio whose sheep and horses had such success that he went to work in Spain. Gallo too made some excellent models from the

55 *Crib Figures by Mosca.*

56 *Four Figures by Sammartino.*

animals he saw in the royal zoo, including the first elephant to be seen in Naples which arrived with a Turkish embassy. The culminating point of Presepio art was reached with Giuseppe Sammartino, and that an artist of his power and reputation should have been ready to devote so much time to the making of Crib figures shows how important they were. Sammartino's interest was in the modelled and painted figure far more than in puppets; he had a tender spot for beggars, and his are as varied as those of the Neapolitan streets. He had a number of followers and pupils and the tradition was so rich, so firmly established, that it has never entirely disappeared.

There is another point that we must notice in the Neapolitan Presepio and that is its connection with contemporary Nativity music. In the eighteenth century Naples was rich in great musicians and the Scarlattis, Pergolesi, Jomelli, Leo, Paisiello all wrote Christmas cantatas, motets, and pastorals intended to be sung in front of the Crib, performed moreover by singers and players from the four famous Conservatori. One composition by Carisena was written in honour of the Presepio in the church of the Jesuits where the Bambino was especially revered. When a Moorish slave of Elisabetta della Rovere refused all efforts to convert him, it was the Santo Bambino who deigned to speak and ever after the converted slave had his place with the shepherds in that particular Crib.

Sicily and Rome

IN SOME ways the Sicilian Crib resembled that of Naples; it too had grown out of Sacre Rappresentazioni, every church and almost every family had its Presepio and one street in Palermo was called the Via dei Bambini, so many were the artists. Some of the figures were puppets, but the greater number were of carved and painted wood, and the clothes were linen dipped in gesso (a special type of plaster) which could be modelled to the exact fold the artist wished, and then painted. These figures were generally smaller than those of Naples and some of them are extraordinarily expressive.

Caltagirone and Trapani were centers of Presepio art with distinguished artists such as Vaccaro, Bongioranni, and Trilocco, and especially Matera who was a poet of the Nativity and also of the countryfolk of Sicily.

The widespread popularity of wood and gesso as materials for figures did not exclude the use of silver gilt, ivory, coral, alabaster, shells, and wax, the latter particularly favoured by Zumbo who also worked in Naples. Beside the Presepio for the rich, there were many others in wood or clay, carved and modelled by the country people for themselves. The Crib can also be seen painted on the gaudy Sicilian carts.

The temperament behind the Sicilian Crib is as different from the Neapolitan as are the songs of the Sulfatari from

*57 The Flight Into Egypt and the House of Nazareth.
Both Are From Sicily.*

those of the Naples fishermen. The Sicilians never greatly fancied the scene in the inn, but they insisted on the Massacre of the Innocents, the Flight into Egypt, and the carpenter shop in Nazareth. In Sicily too shepherds came from the hills "to console the Mother of God"; two always went together alternating the verses of interminable ancient songs with the accompaniment of fiddle, flute, or bagpipe, and it is particularly easy to imagine Sicilian shepherds setting out for the Grotto two thousand years ago.

In Rome Santa Maria Maggiore has always continued as the chief sanctuary of the Nativity, and after it the Ara Coeli acquired renown when it became the home of the Santo Bambino and its Presepio was enriched with a number of figures belonging to an older one in San Francesco a Ripa. Sant' Andrea della Valle, Sant' Antonio, Sts. Cosmas and Damian, Santa Maria in Trastevere were only a few of the churches with famous Presepi, nor were the private enthusiasts much behind those of Naples. It is strange that, given the demand, no names of Roman Crib artists have come down to us. An unfailing characteristic of all Roman Cribs is the presence of a "glory" of angels descending from heaven to earth. One very ambitious Presepio was described by a Dominican Father Labat who travelled in Italy in the eighteenth century: the Crib belonged to a priest who was known as "the Prelate of the Presepio," and different scenes of the Nativity cycle were represented by tableaux in a number of rooms. Naturally the house was always crowded and the Prelate arranged concerts of suitable music in honour of special guests: what could have been better than Corelli's Nativity Concerto or the lovely motets of Nannini; would it not be a good idea to revive them? Wherever there was a Crib there were carols and poems, and in the Ara Coeli

58 *Sicilian Crib by Matera (Eighteenth Century). Now in Munich.*

59 *Santons, Marseilles.*

sermons, too, recited by children while the familiar sounds of the shepherds' bagpipes echoed in the streets. There were other huge Presepi in Palazzo Caffarelli and that arranged by Signor Forti on the top of the Torre dell'Anguillara where the landscape was exactly copied from the view. This Crib was one of the sights of Rome.

Inevitably the southern Presepi absorb our attention, but we must at least remember that in each region of Italy the Crib flourished in churches, in convents, in palaces and cottages, and each reflected local customs and costumes, and was made by local artists using local material.

Among these workers some of the most famous were the "figurinai" of Lucca who have carried, and still carry, their stucco and plaster statuettes all over the world. The craft originated in the Lucchese convents, but it quickly became one of the chief sources of income to the whole district, and among the figures those of the Presepio are never lacking.

The Lombards, on the other hand, gave up the modelled clay figure in favour of figures drawn and painted on paper and stuck on wood, a style perfected by Londonio in the eighteenth century. He was already famous as a painter of country scenes when, after a visit to Rome, he turned his attention to Cribs with which he had great success. His work was carried on by his followers Appiani and Inganni.

It were well worthwhile to pursue the Presepio into every corner of Italy, but we must now turn toward Spain. On the way, Ajaccio in Corsica catches our eye for there, in the room of Madame Mère, is what remains of the Crib played with by the little Bonapartes in 1779 when the small Napoleon removed the Kings' crowns and set them on his brothers' heads while adorning his own person with the Star.

Provence, Spain, and Portugal

IN THE Musée Borély of Marseilles there are three Cribs, Louis XIV, Louis XV, and Louis XVI respectively, which reflect the changing fashions of those reigns. These are Cribs in which delicate china figures play at being shepherds, where the stable has become a court, and the last one recalls the make-believe of the Trianon. The Crèche in France was not as general as in Italy or Germany but it always existed, in churches and in homes, and before it were sung traditional Pastorals.

The Marseillais of the late eighteenth century had a great fancy for mechanical Cribs often combined with a music box, and an ingenious person named Laurent made Cribs to suit contemporary politics. For instance, after the Concordat between Pius VII and Napoleon the Pope could be seen arriving in Bethlehem with the Cardinals and blessing the Holy Family; and in another the Infant Jesus clapped His Hands for the Pope and would turn His head and hold out His arms while the shepherds and Magi passed before Him.

Such tricks, however, soon palled, and attention turned to the clay figures which were being made by a craftsman named Glorian who was followed by Agnel, and then by Antoine and his whole family. They were all modellers who cared nothing for courts and elegance, and a great deal for the people of Provence. The figures were generally small, sometimes tiny and they came to be called Santons while the manger was known as Lou Belen. Before long Marseilles had an annual fair of Santons, and the number of artists increased, and the types and technique varied according to whether the Santon had come from the hands of Pastourel, Boyer, Negre, Fabre, or Guindon. Every Santonnier was concerned in taking all working Provence to Bethlehem, man, woman and child, old and young, some walking, some on donkeys, Guilhéon, Périrour, or Jouan, someone always playing the bagpipes or fiddle. The only set group in a Provençal "Belen" is the Holy Family. The Santon has proved his toughness; he has never become sentimental or romantic or vulgar; he was and is a worker of Provence admitting only two exceptions to his company, "lou Saint Pape" (the holy Pope) and Napoleon.

One cannot speak of Santons and forget the Midnight Mass at Les Baux which still retains echoes of older customs. At the Offertory, to the singing of Provençal Noels an "angel" from behind the altar announces the birth of Christ to the shepherds, and a lamb is brought in on a little cart decked with flowers and lights and drawn by a ram. And Les Baux prides itself on having given hospitality to Balthasar, one of the Magi.

In Spain a magnificent Nativity tradition had been handed down since the Middle Ages in which all the arts took part. Spaniards had always sung of the Nochebuena in carols and songs, had represented it in plays and had built splendid Nativity altars. There were Cribs of the finest goldsmith's art, of ivory, of carved and painted wood, or of clay, Cribs of all sizes and all kinds. Hernandez, Beccerra, Montanes, Cano all made Nativity groups; Pedro Roldan was a maker

60 *Crib in the Ara Coeli Church in Rome* (Felici).

61 *A Spanish Ivory Crib of the Seventeenth Century. Actual size.*

of Cribs of which some may still be extant; and it is said that Lope de Vega owned a Crib with figures of wax. By the seventeenth century the craft of Pesebrista (Crib maker) was actively practised, and employed as many different people as in Naples.

A Crib was made by José Gines for Carlos IV with several scenes in which some of the figures were life size. The chief work of Amadeu, also a great Pesebrista, was the "Nacimento" for San Francisco de Paula in Barcelona, and a fusion of the Neapolitan and Spanish traditions can be found in the workshop of the Salzillo family in Murcia. Nicola Salzillo came to Spain from Capua and with his son Francisco became famous for great groups of the Passion as well as for Cribs. In Spain the tradition of the courtly Crib continued alongside another in which each province represented its own people and customs, and the Spanish Crib had the very great range of the Spanish oversea empire. The missionaries carried it into the heart of the New World and of Asia.

The Crib in Portugal descended from the same great Nativity tradition as in Spain, but at its most elaborate it was restricted to the scenes of the Nativity and the adoration of the Magi. Perhaps owing to less foreign influence Crib making had been deeply rooted in the rustic craft of figures modelled in clay and painted. Such figures appeared alongside of *autos populares* which were performed either by human actors or puppets. Against this background the art of polychrome statuary developed during the sixteenth century, and rather later there were two active centres of Crib making in Lisbon and Mafra.

The numerous Crib artists were often sculptors and undertook commissions for figures of any size; Faustino Rodriguez made most attractive small figures as did also Francisco Elias and Jose Leitas. Jose de Almeida, Policarpo de Silva, and others were all working in and round Lisbon, but the two outstanding names are those of Antonio Ferreira and Machado da Castro. Ferreira and his assistants made a Crib with some five hundred figures for the Basilica of the Coracao de Jesus, and a lovely Crib is Machado da Castro's in Lisbon. It has no genre scenes, no trimmings, no amusing crowd: attention is focussed on the manger in the foreground while beyond the Kings are seen journeying through a very attractive landscape. Here Portuguese Crib art is at its best.

XII

Nineteenth Century — And Now

THE nineteenth century had to be content to echo the
éclat of its predecessor, at least so far as the Southern
countries were concerned. Enthusiastic crowds still went to
see the great Roman and Neapolitan Cribs and good work
was also being done by the Figurari Ceccon, Surdi with
an enormous Presepio, Cifariello, Monteverdi, and Ferrari.

In Germany and Austria there had been a moment of
blight on the Cribs and many of the best ones were sold
piecemeal after the dissolution of the religious orders. However, the Crib had too strong a hold on the German heart
and was not to be dislodged. Crib art recovered itself and
a new school came to the fore headed by Joseph von Fuhrich.
His inspiration came from the early Renaissance, his scenes
were simple and spacious set against a "romantic" background. Every year he produced a new Crib for his own
family, and his work influenced a whole generation.

Johann Berger, Johann Ploderl, Franz Fröhlich, Max
Gehri, Joseph Bachlechner, Andrea Barsam, Wandeln Rei-
ner, and the Lang family carried on the best traditions of
Austrian and German Crib making, and in the middle of
the century the Bozen school culminated in the work of

62 *Czechoslovakian Crib.*

63 *Modern Tyrolese Crib by Joseph Bachlechner,*
Museum for Folk Art, Innsbruck.

Moser. His great Crib, the remains of which are in Munich, was a lifework: it is wood carving and originally it had a quantity of figures, some older ones he had collected, others of his own. Architecture was Moser's chief hobby; never have models been more delicately exact, and as his enthusiasm for different styles varied through the years, his Crib contains some buildings that are Oriental, others Gothic — one was copied from the Hotel de Ville in Brussels — and others again pure Palladian. Moser's unique Crib was saved at least in part by a Crib collector, Doctor Max Schmederer, who found what remained of it in Rovereto. He presented his whole collection containing some excellent examples to the National Museum in Munich, where they can be easily studied but . . . a museum is no home for a Christmas Crib.

Nor did the German production stop with Moser. The Munich sculptor, Sebastian Osterrieder, gave up his whole career to it and spent several years in Palestine studying the landscape and background: Bradl, Zehentbauer, Unterpieringer, Gammerler, Lechner-Hall are among the more modern Crib makers, using a great variety of material and many designs.

Besides these Cribs made by artists in all the German-speaking lands, and notably too among the Czechs there has always been the traditional Crib of the countryside. The more sophisticated Czech Crib usually came from Iglau, Zwittau, or Schlucknau where there were outstanding craftsmen, and they were given to inserting models of famous buildings into their backgrounds, while for their own pleasure the Czechs, like the Austrians and the Poles, were warm patrons of the Krippenspiel which journeyed from place to place, always sure of its audience, a long-lived, poor relation of the Mystery stage and the Puppet theatre. It generally

64 Polish Szopka. In Poland the Crib Often Formed Part of
a Marionette Show (Appetiti).

65 *The Visit of the Magi. From the Congo (Dessena).*

66 *A Chinese Crib (Appetiti).*

had three stages one above the other; on the lowest was the Crib which carried the stationary group of the Crib, on the second the guilds and trades were shown in action, and on the topmost tier was the Krippenstadt on which a regular play was acted with all kinds of rowdy scenes and fun.

In Poland the Szopka, which was a variety of Krippenspiel, was enormously popular, and though the Crib had its place in churches, it was the Szopka which carried it through the countryside gathering up local Nativity customs and carols.

*   *   *

Our little sightseeing trip through Crib history has brought us to our present century which is as surprising as any other. Even fifty years ago there was little to suggest that the English, who seemed to have definitely turned their backs on the Crib, should reappear on the scene full of enthusiasm. I do not know whether, during penal times English Catholics kept to the practice of the Crib; naturally since the emancipation our churches have had their Cribs and have been emulated increasingly by the Anglo Catholics. But this is not all: Cribs are now in great demand in hospitals, institutions, in a variety of public buildings, and many of the big shops devote a window to the Crib. A life size Crib is set up in Trafalgar Square, the heart of London, and the Christmas Poster Campaign, run by a group of adventurous Catholics is fast spreading to all the English-speaking lands.

All over the United States we see the same thing happening. A quarter century ago a crib was a rarity in the American home — except perhaps for families of German or Italian extraction. Today it has taken its place, with the Christmas tree, in a large number of Catholic homes, and in non-Catholic ones as well. Many people everywhere realize that the Crib is one

67 *Nativity Group in Terra Cotta by Robert C. Koepnich,*
Dayton Art Institute.

68 *Christmas Crib, St. Luke's Church, River Forest, Ill., by*
Frederick Doyle. Design and Figures Are of American Origin.

69 *Crib Designed After Paintings and Drawings of Albrecht Dürer.*
Formerly in the Convent of Our Lady of the Pines, Fremont, Ohio.

70 *Crib in St. Anne's*
Church, Fremont,
Ohio. Designed by
Rev. Aloysius S. Horn.
The Figures Were
Carved in Italy.

71 *Outdoor Crib. Designed by Charles Williams for the City of Cincinnati, Ohio.*

72 *An American-Mexican Crib in Our Lady of Guadalupe Church, Toledo, Ohio.*

of the most eloquent protests against the tide of materialism which is trying to cut the cable between the celebration of Christmas and the Nativity of Our Lord Jesus Christ. In the United States the movement to "Put Christ Back Into Christmas" must be given some credit for this realization. The cry is now for Cribs, and once again Crib artists are being offered a big chance.

It is happening, too, all over Europe, and in Spain, Italy, and Germany there exist Societies of the Friends of the Crib which are particularly useful in keeping Crib lovers in touch and whose publications offer practical help to the amateur who wants to do something more exciting than to buy his Crib ready made.

Some years ago an International Congress of Crib Lovers was organized in Rome by the foremost Italian connoisseur of Cribs, Signor Angelo Stefanucci, and at the same time there was a most interesting exhibition of Cribs from all over the world. Very surprising some of them were, and one point that can hardly have escaped any visitor is the necessity of helping the production of Cribs in our missions.

The Crib is never stereotyped, its variety is endless: Bethlehem is the only place where all peoples meet as brothers: Christmas without Christ is the emptiest, saddest vanity of the world: the Christmas Crib alone is Christmas.

Christmas Crib Societies

United States of America. American Christmas Crib Society, 305 South Wayne Street, Fremont, Ohio.
Argentina. Hermandad del Santo Pesebre, Buenos Aires.
Brazil. Associacão de Presipistas, 78 Jardin Paulistano, San Paulo.
Chile. Grupo de Pesebristas de la Asociacion Folklorica Chilena, Cariba 9764.
Austria. Verband der Krippenfreunde Oesterreichs, Pfarrplatz 6, Innsbruck.
Germany. Vereins Bayrischer Krippenfreunde, Balanstrasse 9, Amberg, Munich. Landesgemeinschaft der Krippenfreunde im Rheinland und West-Falen, Ubierstrasse 21, Bad Godesberg, Köln. Krippenfreunde "Gloria," Sedanstrasse 82, Remscheid. Kreis der Krippenfreunde fur Berlin und Ostdeutschland Am Waldhaus 28–30, Berlin-Kikolassee (Protestant).
Italy. Associazione Italiana Amici del Presepio, Via Madonna dei Monti 84, Rome.
Spain. Asociacion de Pesebristas de Barcelona, Canuda 35. Asociacion de Belenistas de Madrid, Trafalgar 14. Asociacion de Belenistas de Pamplona, Calle Beunza 32.

The Association in Barcelona is particularly active and in 1952 instituted the Universalis Foederation Praesepistica which keeps in touch with other Crib Societies. With the object of increasing the diffusion of the Crib an international congress was held in Rome in 1954, and another is announced in Barcelona for 1957.

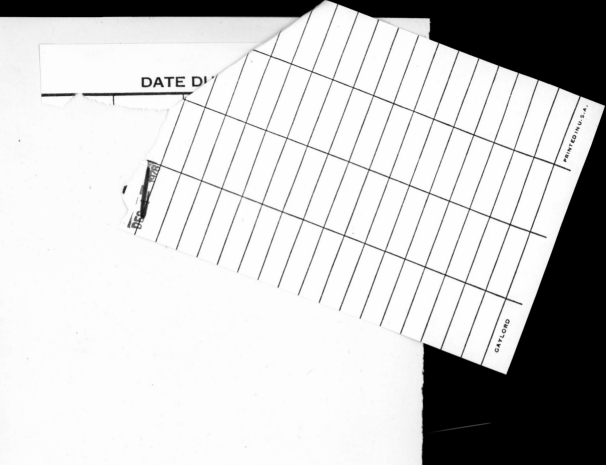